Table of Contents

Can you find these words?

drums

hair

jump

splash

I Can Move

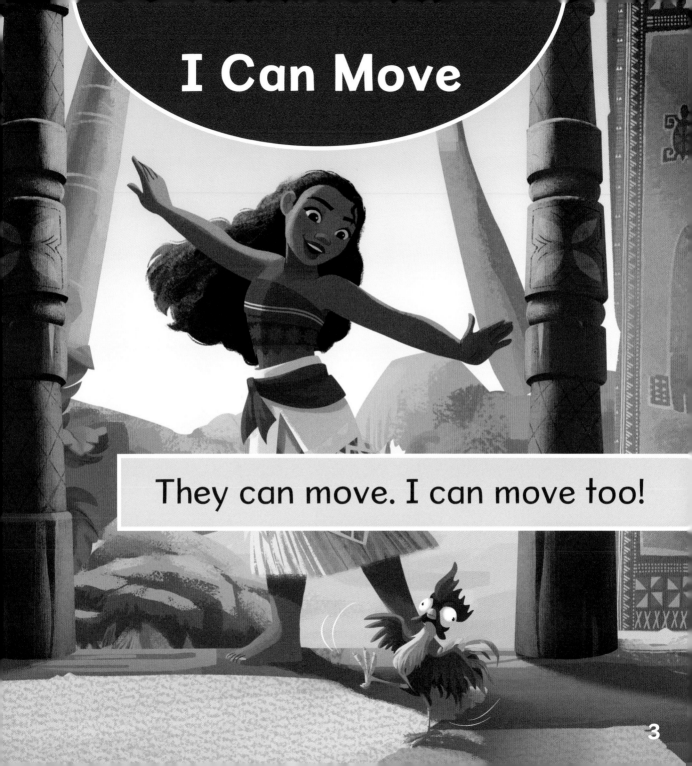

They can move. I can move too!

Moana can play the **drums**.

drums

4

I can play the drums.

Tiana can dance with a friend.

I can dance with a friend.

Ariel can **splash**.

splash

I can splash.

Mulan can **jump** high.

jump

I can jump high.

Rapunzel can swing on her **hair**.

hair

12

I can swing on a swing set.

Did you find these words?

drums

hair

jump

splash

Picture Glossary

 **drums** (druhmz): Percussion instruments with the shape of a cylinder that make a sound when you hit them.

 **hair** (hair): The thin, soft strands that grow from people's heads.

 **jump** (juhmp): To push off with your legs and feet to move into the air.

 **splash** (splash): To throw or scatter liquid so that it falls in drops.

Index

About the Author

Hailey Scragg is a writer and editor from Ohio. She likes to walk her dog to get moving. She also enjoys reading, cooking, and writing books for children.

Published by Rourke Educational Media. No part of this book may be reproduced or utilized in any form or by any means, electronic or mechanical including photocopying, recording, or by any information storage and retrieval system without permission in writing from the publisher.

www.rourkeeducationalmedia.com

PHOTO CREDITS: cover: Shutterstock (insets); pages 5, 7, 9, 11: Shutterstock; page 13: GettyImages, ©Jaren Wicklund

Edited by: Hailey Scragg
Cover and interior design by: Lynne Schwaner

Library of Congress PCN Data
I Can Move / Hailey Scragg
ISBN 978-1-73164-323-0 (hard cover)(alk. paper)
ISBN 978-1-73164-235-6 (soft cover)

Library of Congress Control Number: 2020945611

Printed in the United States of America
01-3502011937